Little Fish

Lorrie Goldensohn

FOMITE
BURLINGTON VT

ISBN-13: 978-1-959984-53-5
Library of Congress Control Number: 2024938393

Fomite
58 Peru Street
Burlington, VT 05401
06/11/2024

Barry Nathan Goldensohn

1937-2023

Acknowledgements

"Usufruct," "Women Say This, Say That," "Our Father Abraham," "Wedding in A Field," and from "The Swimmer": "The Stroke," "The Poet," "Hands," "The Hospital,' "Why," "Where Are You," and "Weeping," from *Salmagundi*

"Dirt Dust Dinginess And Contamination" and "Calculus of Death," on-line magazine, *Molly Bloom* (UK)

"Lament for the Makaris," *The Yale Review*

"Hermit Thrush," "Little Fish," *Poet Lore*

"I Lay," *The New Republic*

"Enfield Calling East Long Pond," *The Birch Song Anthology 2*, (2019)

"Animals, too," from *Roads Taken*, eds. Sydney Lea, Chard de Niord

Contents

I

II

III

IV
The Swimmer

LITTLE FISH

Even this upland lake might flood—
the shoreline hemlock
erect under clear water so many feet down.
Their fern-like tips waiting to tickle
the feet of the divers who will come later, after we
who once lived here, no longer
grope for the blocked water line or the lost
sunglasses slipped from the dock:

fog loosening our brains as the decades
continue their heap heap heap upon us.

*

I have finished knitting a perfectly brilliant sock.

*

Although the local winter has been kind,
the weather continues uncertain upon our return.

*

We went away. Came back. A feeling
wriggles to consciousness, its
contours spilling across—what
is the word for it?

Lost. Never mind. The point
is the crackle of joy, little fish
breaking from its flap of lake water.

Man in a Red Canoe

He sits there in the red canoe
the sun splashing him with a thick
glaze of yellow
his fists raise the paddle
to dip again, again

transparent drops
fall from the paddle

while below the distant tree line
the spread water
inverts and repeats
every bit of the loved geometry

Somewhere at his feet
the rod is ready; trout

leap after the rising flies

An Arab proverb tells me
Allah does not subtract
from a lifetime
the days that a man
spends fishing. This man.

HERMIT THRUSH

Plick: plick, then *plick*. I hear
you turn the pages in the other
lamplit room. After the loon
has ceased his whinny, its echo
growing over water, you
cannot imagine our companionable
silence. Strung between us
on the rope of today's hours
in which I heard the steady
whack of the hammer on the screen door,
fixing the loose hang that nagged us
season after season. And then
steps going out to the dock,
after which you called me
to come and hear the hermit thrush—
who hides in deep woods
although we hear the damp
pearling of his gift song at dusk,
when the air vibrates
with the drill and sting of insects.
Moths strike the glass or screen—
their bodies flaming out for me
in my larger light. We know
how long the moths get to live,
in pitiless ratio to their size—but
what about the hermit thrush?
Opaque in his dressing of leaves
and feathers. Tiny lice
smaller than he may cling to him.

ELMORE

Elmore Leonard says
if it sounds like *writing* take it out.

How can he not know
some of my best hours on earth
have been spent in reading *writing*?

Luscious. Unnecessary. Words
apoplexing on the page, collecting
like the thrush that just alit
on the outermost tip of the elderberry branch—
shaking it as he leaves—leaves, feathers,
a pulsation of skin and hollow bone lifting.

Do not own every book you like.
Thing thing and thing—years in gathering.
Stuffed into every room of our house,

they litter the bathroom floor,
brown-blotched with coffee and tea spill—
they also oil up good on the kitchen table.
Left with the open pages
that faced the rain on the porch,
I try not to wince
at the ruffled mess they dry into.

I am my underlinings in soft pencil.
Books take up all that space in the basement
even after my back breaks,
hauling ten cartons out to the car
for the yearly sale at the town library:
from a thousand paper cuts, my mind
undergoes tiny hemorrhages,
my past bleeding out the door with them.

Wedding in a Field

In the green glade, salt sweat
breaks over hot skin, our clothes
beginning to stick, as we walk

from the cooled car to the wedding.
We cross toward the people we know,
our eyes covertly engaging
the groom's men, and his family,

soon to be ours. Seating ourselves
gingerly on the folding chairs,
we wobble into the soft turf,
and shush the small child asking

Where is the "altar"? —There.
In the wilting circle of wildflowers
where the bride stands, blinding us
with the white sheath of her dress,

her tanned shoulders and ample breasts
upthrust: a docile sweetness in her smile.
Her hand shades her eyes
from the cutting sun, as she waits

for her father, sweltering in his ceremonial suit,
and reading, in a low, hesitant voice,
words for the looming *later*, kind
and fearful words for her happiness.

Beside the bride, the matron of honor
in dress heels, tall, inscrutable;
the practiced chignon of her graying hair
pulling her temples and her mouth tight,

opening wide her dark-water eyes.
Our dimpled, effervescent bride will never have
this faint tincture of unhappiness;
nor will the sturdy bridegroom now in shadow

ever need to hold hard and fast
like the white-haired, bent-kneed husband,
rocking slightly on his heels,
and carrying the sum of himself

with such wary doubtfulness.
I ask you to glance
at these older people
alighting among us, as they pause

from a long leave-taking journey west,
giving their own oak bedstead
to the young couple now promising,
in sweating serge and stiffened satin,

never to fuck anyone but each other:
which we witness,
while the gift bed waits,
dismantled and roped on the roof of the car.

Nimitz Trail

The coral flash of a girl's running shoes
are flicking towards me:
                              ahead, the little
twist of that toddler's neck, a crisp
of sunlight streaking her profile
within the canvas hood of her stroller,

bouncing in front of her bouncing,
panting, pushing dad. The toddler
looks back, checking for him.

Why are you so joyless?

Big in your episodic speech to me,
the bruised elbow, or was it the pulled
muscle in your left calf—or
some other damned injury natural
to your age and its bodily deployments. It is

not my friend who is dying
who catches you, his beautiful
face laid back on the cushion
of his terrible easy chair,
                              a face
full of suppressed suffering—

after all you have never known him—
he does not come to mind.

Nor is it say the news photo
of some weeks back,
a child brought up from the well,
a dead child where you can see
the wide gash in its throat

washed all too clean.
                        I charge you
in the teeth of what we see
to be happy. Complain a little less.

THREE'S COMPANY

Chana, you are causing big swatches
of my sleep to come undone, leaving me
abashed at what I at the last

did not send your way: forgive me.
I need to hear your gnarly treble, its little

catches, aloud—trying to hitch the brave
gay ferocity of your final months
to these lines…Let your wit, sweetened,

take David to the piano—the ringing
baritone, deft pedal on Cole Porter, black eyes
smoldering beneath the jagged chic

of his thick hair, later so white, whoops—
Chana—put your hand lightly over his mouth!
muting those great whoppers he used to tell.

Then bring in Leonard: his splayed feet
marching, elbows aloft. Winters in Berkeley,
he said whole poems to us by heart. Low

and beautiful the vibrancy of his voice…
Up, then down the hills of Tilden Park, phrase
by phrase, he gave me Borges' *Everness*, huge

sonorous words I could not learn from him,
to this day I have to look them up:
Dios, que salva el metal, salva la escoria,

y cifra en Su profetica memoria—What?
("Store…in Your prophetic memory…") All three
of you dead the same year. Leonard. The wheels

of his old bike dawdling down a college path,
his arms latching me to the crossbar, his breath
tickling my ear—a chaste moment. But pungent.

In each emptying year that comes, each tick
of the late night clock—I fear you will all
sleep in me more soundly…Wake up! Wake up!

I want so badly to talk to you.

LAMENT FOR THE MAKARIS
Homage to William Dunbar

In health and lonely sickness the victrola comforted me,
Winding round and round until it wound down,
And then the thing had to be cranked up
So that the glorious voice would not wobble and quaver
Or the Blue Danube run down, in *softe sommer*, as it
Orbited the grass, there in Long Island,
Leaving me in fear of the death of joy.

And where are you collecting now, my old LPs?
Slickly ten or twelve inch, you were
A black thread encircling the heart,
Only Victoria of the Angels knew how far
You could swing me, riding out, and then yet
Farther out--on one note, and then the next—each
Sweetness leaving me in fear of the death of joy.

And where are you? Store with the wide aisles I patrolled,
Eyeing the delicious, glamour-coated boxes, each
More ardently coveted than the next, O Fischer-Dieskau,
Where are you, each of your performances in place
No longer: the shelves stuffed to a different tune,
A different singer, the marquee given over,
The management deaf to the death of my joy.

This fals world is but transitory, its flapping sheet music,
Its pianola rolls, also the black vinyl in the extremity
Of its shine—even the brown, overheated audiotapes uncoiling
In their cases as the hapless fingernail fails to spool them back,
They join the cracked cds wending their way to landfill,
The bent antennae of all those radios not spared to linger,
They too shake silently in fear of the death of joy.

The stait of man dois change and vary.
The pianist with only one good hand after the war
Has come to rest, he takes no more taxis, he lies down
In the dirt with the rest of the dead musicians,
The rest of the silenced instruments, banished
From the chambers where the white-stringed earbuds rule, while
A greyhaired audience weeps in fear of the death of joy.

Marjorie tucking in her Sunday skirt, seats herself at the upright—
Before she moved, unmercifully, a continent away from me.
Four-hand Mozart on the rack, sherry bottle on the lid, two glasses—
Our fingers, un-arthritic, now swept into the bin beyond recycle.
Husbands and children scatter before us, while we laugh
In our fearless racket, slow on the fast notes, fast on the slow—
Deaf, dumb, and dead now, the making of that joy.

Usufruct

"The earth belongs in usufruct to the living…the dead have neither powers nor rights over it…"

Thomas Jefferson

If earth belongs to the living
then what is the place of the dead?
Or yet more perplexing,
of those who are dying…

Dying on a pallet in the schoolhouse,
a boy wrapped in the overwhelming
stench of his wound.

Dying in the ditches both fast and slow
after the squadron passes.

The blood of so many killed in my name
acrid in my nostrils
close to my living face.

Closing a book with a tattered cover,
I shut away a dead person's words.

Although they still belong to me.

Licking the flap,
I seal a dead person's photo
in the tomb of an envelope.

I give away a pink coat
once worn by my dead mother—
I think her smell clings to it—
and put my flowers in her blue glass bowl.

BOOKLIFE

At first it was never about writers
or even writing. I was not
encouraged to read: *"Girl,*
get your head out of that book!"
my uncle shouted. I was not
thinking about "literature": I read
as a gambler gambles, as a drinker
drinks. I never bothered much
about the bunch of bearded men
in dingy photos, or how
they made it all up: it was
their high-colored people I meant
to be or meet: placed in my nest
of books, I lay awake, but dreaming:
not so much to be loosened
from my own life as in this
spaceless space to add to it…
the use of Me or Not Me not yet
existing; young, I knew
how much completion lay
insistently ahead.
                    At the National
in London, I stood at Meindert Hobbema,
before his *Avenue in Middelharnis*,
its frontal wedge of deeply rutted road
calling out from where it crazily
dove forward to the horizon—
which lay only two-fifths up the canvas—
the road ceasing at the edge where it
disappeared into that huge Dutch sky.

For how many minutes did I,
no longer a child, try to walk
into it? On each side of the road

the brown ditchwater. Early spring:
the brown fields. The funny
17th century clothes—on tiny pedestrians
their skirted coats. Smudge of dog.
A man fixing hops alongside. Make sure
to look at the skinny trees, naked
verticals swaying in the central
clump of the wide horizon, plastered
at their tips with fizzy leaves. Again
I squeeze my eyes to dizzy slits,
trying to enter my foot
onto that rutted road.

                        On the colorless
neutrality of the page, there are
no objects; no appearances massing
between me and the life
held in such reserve...a sheet of letters
so nothing. But quite marvelous,
the stageful of reality these spindled
black bundlings manage to serve: their
terms invisible, their voices silent,
except when sounded—down
at the bottom here, in the final

line, you can hear me faintly, yes?

TALKING BOOKS, CIRCA 1985

i
Side by side, our parlor on wheels rolled us
from the Cabot Highlands to Machias Bay;
while you drove, I tended the sound, as if
we flanked the conjugal hearth, the usual book
at hand—only here, the pages turn themselves
as I feed tapes to the deck, instead of logs
to the fire. Our heads at complementary angles,
tipped to the rich English of the voice issuing
from the speakers of our car.
                                        The A.C. on—
our windows closed—ears channeling the words
that carry us beyond the mown fields, the riverbank,
past cows and creamy clouds—my stocking feet
propped on the audio cassettes cache-ing
a full twenty hours of *Jane Eyre*. "I was obliged,"
she is saying, "to yield." Prompted by Charlotte,
prompted by our reader: "I was shaken from head
to foot with acute distress…" Her man
teasing her with leave-taking, testing her
with the bogus installation of Blanche Ingram
as his bride, waiting to spring on her the news
that only she is the true Intended.
                                        How each
will pay for his sorry tricks! Before Miss Bronte
works her dazzling restitution. All through
Jane's bursting tears, the nightingale
sings at dusk in Thornfield Orchard. August
sun blazes steadily through our windshields,
two lanes and then four lanes of freeway
parting beneath our wheels, while the shy
governess crosses custom, sweeping aside
the dress of her mortal flesh to say to Mr. Rochester:
"It is my spirit that addresses your spirit—"

Until he folds her in his arms, making plain
to plain Jane how much he loves her.

Tears rill in the corners of my eyes:
crossing into Maine, my nose wrinkles
at the stink of the Androscoggin,
while we come upon the moment
when the governess not only sends love out
but on that twilight bench receives it.

ii
When Mrs. Gaskell met Miss Bronte, one
novelist meeting another, she guessed her
a half-head shorter than herself, noting her
"very good and expressive" eyes—but
could not omit the mouth, "many teeth gone"—
or the broad brow, "rather overhanging":

Charlotte at thirty-four, compelling most
through her musical voice, the ardor of which
even now we cannot settle within the meager
defiant little frame.
                            Journey and yearning
share so much of the sounds of each other—
spirit, flesh, and the hand that holds the pen—
journey and yearning, writing the panting
and mobile sounds of the animal soul—
as the animal self, unstoppable, appears
in its career of wanting.
                            A golden retriever
juts his head far out the window of the car ahead,
which shimmies on a wide curve; the dog
rights himself, then scrambles on unseen feet,
his fine eyes turning to us and then the road.

iii
Late summer lights up the shoppers

in the main streets, spilling onto the crowded
parking lots in the tourist malls,
our speakers momentarily shut down
by the rapper's blast from the convertible
pulling alongside.
                    We know how Charlotte,
exiled to a Yorkshire parlor, waited
for the letters that never came, no answer
to their angry, unbearable pleadings…
She nursed her father's weak eyes,
and lowered her own to write *Jane Eyre.*

We unwrap our sandwiches in the car,
gingerly hold our scalding coffee
poured into too thin paper cups, as the voice
in steady exhalation thrums before us,
a curious, coordinate,
and bodiless prompt: five more hours

in the trance of listening,
before the denouement burns itself
right through to where the doubled,
coupled front-seat body stirs—one half
in traffic at the wheel, one half
manning the knobs—our flesh, sidereal,
linking us to the one book, climaxing
before the climax of arrival—
will this be All? Our muscles stiff,
we stretch out legs and arms before
we take our parcels from the car,
our eyes having to re-focus:
"Reader, I married him." Ending
one sort of thing to begin another.

II

Lunch Time Quartet

that little
burn of contact, nudging
your arm in the seat beside me, the touch
enough to tell you how happy
the wide-faced, little blonde violinist
makes me—visibly dancing in place,
the swerve of her shoulders
the frequent shifting of her body's axis—
look how she nods quickly
to the broad hipped violist
for whom she steadies the beat

the weaving
jut of instruments allowing my eye
to map
what my ear must open

music splashing our faces
the drops
almost
painfully wrung

you knew what I meant by touching you
I knew that you would know

East Long Pond Vt 05467 Calling Enfield EN20QT

As conversations go it was quite a good one
Adjusting a nervous Skype we hunched in close

so that in Enfield they might see us back-lit
by the sunset of our pond the day after the bomb

hit Parsons Green on the District Line
But they and theirs were safe, a quiet night

spread from the halo of their parlor lamp
onto the sofa where they fiddled with the laptop

until both their heads could fit the screen
as intimately as ours did

Undeterred they had stepped out
for Open House in their "Ancient Village"

where down the brick path to the Council garden
they surveyed the 800-year-old Minchenden oak

O my it is ugly—I thought, seeing their picture—
a listing robot on a bad hair day! A slatted bench

circles the monster almost-stump whose girth
once measured well over 27 feet,

although now it has shrunk some
still lifting its sky-hooking branches

so heavy they keep on falling off—leaving
on the re-fattening trunk the large oval scars

of their steady drop to the ground
The Minchenden oak began around Magna Carta

I was so happy us old people could just
talk companionably, putting the lives of terror

to the side   The river of mentionables
coursing high and steady

keeping our deaths from rushing over
and killing us one by one on the spot

I Lay

At dawn I lay
in the warm
nest of the bed sheets

trying to recover the sound
the beat, the scatter
of a child's feet   running

I said Funny
You said Sssh
still half asleep

But I was groping for the lost
whether it was the boy
or whether it was the girl

Many years ago
we had one of each

FOR ALICE

I am sorry we cannot become friends.
I woke up last night on fire with shame
that I had grudged speech with you
while you were still alive. When you were
dead, after the first decades I forgave
what there was to be forgiven.
Next decades, as you became
one of the long-term dead, I began
to see how I loved you—not just
in the little ways of childhood
but even into the difficult years
when I became your grown daughter.
But liking you? To me, you seemed
a simple soul. In the chaos of first
parenthood, when we lived in your attic,
messy with our new baby, once
past midnight, dead with sleeplessness,
I ran barefoot onto the lawn, yelling
grievance at my young husband—milk
spilling in my breasts, as rearing up
like a startled animal, I saw you: apparition
in your frilly nightgown, roused from sleep
by our quarreling, approaching me to say,
"You must plan more regular mealtimes."
Then something yet more general. I forget
your exact words, but not their absurdity.
Life gave you an innocent, but stubborn
intelligence, without my kniving
introspection—both my children loved you:
also my man. And how engrossing
my friends found your stories, Mittel-Europa,
the busy person-rich household, a comfy
comic childhood with pets, at nightfall
when you were five, Hänschen

trotting you safely home,
fast asleep in the little blue pony cart—
then war, and the adult descent into pain,
until betrayed by one continent
onto another, you wrapped it up—
we all lurched forward—
into the little house on Sylvia Street.
A linden tree standing in front, *lime-tree*
in English, and in Coleridge,
this lime-tree bower, my prison—
encased beneath its down-turning branches I, too,
Silent with swimming sense.

Pee Pot & Sour Milk

Pee pot & sour milk. They scented
that early railroad flat when we lived
in Spanish Harlem. Outside in the hall
the pail where the dirty diapers got put
for the pickup service my mother-in-law
so generously allotted. Inside

the plastic bathinette in which I dunked
my colicky baby, still screaming
even as the water touched her—
the frightened, tense recoil of her little body
rests in my fingers—sixty years later.
Having put her in the bath at 2 am

because I didn't know what else to do.
Having tried everything in my short
book of maternal tricks. One lamp
lit the darkness—how alone I was with her
and how exhausted. It seems a kind of grace
that she grew up loving the water. Loving

the dare of ocean, lake, pond, and river—
athough my mothering mattered a lot, gratefully
I cannot say that it meant everything.
When the fresh diapers came, they smelt
so good, the linen crisp and white,

that my hands put on her little butt.

Women Say This, That

Casual and cruel, its delivery
hurt me the most.
You meant to hurt.

I parsed
and re-parsed
your taunt in my mind:

the blunt facts of my childhood
flung at me
as if I
were somehow responsible
for the damage
they made in me.

Of course I am responsible.

As if my life did not near daily
bring the old record back.
As if I never knew
my lack
growing in the shade of those

unstoppable abandonments
made by those who could not
help themselves—as if

I did not know
could never see—
how the thumb of my injuries
pressed on others' eye
including, somewhat

to the rear of my attachments: you

After all these years
how absent forgiveness.
I smile. You smile.
Come, give me your usual kiss.

BLOOD

At dawn, I bought fresh pineapple—
an hour later placing it on the kitchen counter,
my left hand stuck clumsily
on its wobbly bottom, awaiting
the knife that in my right hand,
instead of the pineapple,
laid my fingertip open—

blood all over the sink—but not
on the pineapple.
                    Dawn
had seen me, market day in Waialua,
idling by bags of local peanuts,
tall orchids lifting their spray—
drifting from stall to stall,
and pausing at the long and curly
Chinese beans. My father's people

stooped in the pineapple fields,
came to California, then
crossed the mainland to halt
in me—my half Filipino body
standing in its phenotype

to be met by a young vendor
handing over my dew-wet
kale and lettuce
and calling me *Auntie*. I didn't
not like that. It
hit with a pleasing astringency.
Because I still carry
the short legs flat fanny
and the ambiguous
color of my skin

which matters—how much? The

epicanthine eyelid. Mine. Catcalls,
jeering children running after me. That is
so far behind me, even farther,

a dead man—has he
a shirt to his deeply-brown back?
Bent over in a sun-struck field;
his small, tapered hands,
the shape of mine, the fingers
quick-stripping green beans from the row
at his knees: he is
an uncle—or possibly my father.

WEDDING DRESS

I did it in seven minutes—in the Sixties,
a decade after we married. Mini-skirts
had just come in. Dust motes
spinning in the light, close and hot
in my mother's attic, the silky, checked
cloth the color of pewter and smoke,
where it rose to my hand in folds, still
unsuitable as a wedding dress—both mother
and mother-in-law had agreed on that—
but they humored my pick, afraid
of the backlash of my twenty-year-old tongue.

Downstairs, slipping the dress
over the thinned body I'd won back
in a recent diet, I turned and twisted,
and gathered the dress up into my hands:
taking the shears, I lopped away its ample hem.
What made me think I could fix
or even re-use my dated, ritual gown?

Then I looked in the mirror
at the gray aborted skirt, now a silly
double palm's width above my knees.
Tearing it off me, cramming the wounded thing
back in the Bonwit Teller box—box
and dress both disappearing forever—
I cut the dress, but kept the husband.

                        In Brooklyn,
my very first time in shul, I stood before the rabbi,
a white-feathered pillbox pushed on my reluctant head.
How good I looked, they said. A white veil

halfway down my halfway Asian face.

I choked back giggles when the rabbi's mouth
opened in front of me, and from him the loud,
frightening holy noise came out—startled,
my eyes and unruly nose watering simultaneously,
tears and snot clotting the veil,
as the huge prayer passed me
in the cut of an instant from bride to wife.

NATIVE SPEECH

How odd to hear my mother
laugh—a ringing
pleasure at her cousin's joke,
every German nuance accessible to her;—
her freshly-flown-in kin from Chicago,
newly-introduced to me,
telling my marveling mother
such a funny piece of news.
Not translated for me—

although she once raised her right hand
next to a courtroom flag
and declared allegiance
in American English.

My mother's laugh came after the war,
after the flag.
Aunts and cousins settled well past
the throes of disaster. Who
was at the door? an aunt had wondered,
when the uncle fell inside
beaten by chains wielded in an alleyway.
Which cousin was it? in stocking feet
who fled over the rooftops to Amsterdam.
In my family the lengthy geographies of escape,
the shorter ones of capture.

My mother's English never a match
for the dark and heavy life overtaking her
right here in the New World.

In the Old World, a black and white
group on a picnic blanket—
a young Tante Lore, a cousin Annie,

smiles darkening
beneath their wide straw brims—they
pause
before the wine glasses lift

My mother's voice
keeps the neat impress of its early vowels.

Her missing jokes reach out to me
from deep inside another planetary track—
showing how much
stays cut from the second tongue,

going back to where the first things learned
had shared names:
where mother, father, brothers and cousins
said *table*,
said *chair* or *bed*, and laughed alike.

PORTRAIT

You had two names, one
used outside the family—*Alice*
to rhyme with *malice*—and then
the prettier one, *Ahleese*, a sound
with no American counterpart.
Your voice pleasantly low, but to me,
embarrassingly accented...

A woman taking oral histories
decided courage was your distinction.
Ah—but that myopic
animal loyalty to den and cub:
I was the resentful cub.

You beguiled so many.
Those dinners still tasting in memory,
the pink pursed mouth,
the bent head, listening...Now

that you are safely dead and cannot
adlib to me the terse, familiar judgments,
I play the tapes you recorded, hear
incredulously the little snort,
the giggle overcoming you
at an irrepressibly comic turn...
halting you on the way
to some really bad outcome.

The members of your large household?
mother with the keys, father
who yelled at you only once,
mother's mother with the ample lap,
father's mother who carped, father's
maiden sister—she left no impression—

two older brothers, one you loved,
one you did not—and then you, in that

photo I hang in my hall: you are
plump, and I think plain, standing
in that scrubby Rhineland pasture,
your face cuddling with the broad neck
of the mare you sat with over long nights
in the stable, a handful of straw, and then
a handful of oats, before her fever broke!
One of your best stories—Edith, *die Itsa.*
(Not *die* Itsa as in *die hard*, but *die* as in *diesel.*)

An unseen hand reaches around the mare's head,
the other tensing slightly, fist closing
over the rope of an improvised bridle.
Her flanks are still skeletal—her skinny legs
brace—sweetly you lean into each other. You

have a white blouse, black stockings,
and a dark skirt shows your sturdy shoes.
Thick, and soft your bobbed hair…Tomboy

who pleaded with the yardmen
to let you ride the wildest horses,
while you ruined the handmade lace dresses
in the mud of barns and stables.

You wrote of your "unfortunately"
protected life: first father, and when
he died, the favored elder brother.

"Protected" was not the word
your younger brother used.
My cousins said their father said
his little sister was spoiled rotten.

Spoiled rotten! But how life broke you:
took your life decade by decade
and almost shook it to bits:
punishment in excess of all flaw.

My Mother's Face in Rapid City, SD

Was that the trip coming east or the one
going west?

              No place to put
the big purse with the lace handkerchief,
let alone the pillowy grandmother herself
packed in the back seat with them—

two under five sleeping or whining
or getting carsick

the boy holding aloft the teeny plastic
Chevy whose wheels he drives
across the girl's arm, who
flinches and wails "It's touching me"

My mother pleading with us to stop
Each motel as we fled past igniting
her despair which we in the front seat

ignored.   To soothe her we said
we'll stop in Rapid City

Your hands painted to the driver's wheel
your feet tippy tapping from clutch
to gas pedal to brake and back.

Memory does not conceal the midnight
moment we wheeled into Rapid City
motel after motel flush with the men
building missile silos
whiskey glasses sliding down the bars
red lights flashing everywhere
the crash of movement, trucks and cars

humped into all available parking

One desk clerk after the other sending us on
So we pulled out the air mattresses—pumped them
and stacked the Oma with the kids in the car
while we spread out on the gravelly dirt
which was the gift of Turtle River Park

Wakened near dawn by heavy rain
my mother's face grimly waiting
for us to notice the water
puddling in our deflated sleeping bags

and then
the cold trek over muddy planking
to the only open café

As we gaggled in
the faces swiveled around
to watch us be told
how there was no flush toilet or hot water

and they were out of eggs too

My mother's face
which did not increase its frown
or get carsick or whine but which let us
feel the lash of her silent disapproval
which she swung
against the full fruit of our folly
standing in the judgment of God
which had fallen on us in Rapid City

She too
now one with the mud   her ashes
cast in the waters of an eastern lake

the stone of memory blocking my mouth
so that I scarcely   breathe

III

OUR FATHER ABRAHAM

Abraham walks in a stupor,
His dream-driven feet lifting
Without volition up to the summit:

a cruel trick.
After all the talk of covenant
to have to take his little son
on such a journey—

but God will not loose him.
With such innocence
Isaac looks to his father and asks
where the lamb for the sacrifice
might be?

In a terror of hope
Abraham answers, *God will provide.*

God *tempted* Abraham.
(Why ever should our book
Treat *tempt* and *test* as the same?)

On Mount Moriah Abraham
binds the late-born Isaac
lays the cloven wood upon him,
takes up the fire,
and stretches forth his hand—

We dress in the blood of Abraham's obedience.

Although a ram appeared in the nearby thicket,
and Abraham
re-directed his blade,
I think for no longer than the momentary

sheep shape of mercy
should we let this God live.

CALCULUS OF DEATH

Death is neither mother nor brother.
Death does not count as a family member
Although it joins all families.

Here is how you do not count.
Here is how you may not assign numbers to Death.

Marek Edelman died in his nineties
Living an exemplary life in war in peace.

Josef Mengele did not.
Josef died too in his nineties
Enjoying health. As to his example?
Do not think of it, the cunning
Butcher of Auschwitz.

When Marek Edelman went
To the Umschlagplatz, empowered
To de-select sick Jews from the camp trains
He took the healthy, and though
Her mother begged for her life

He passed over a fourteen year-old
To select Zosia for the last spot remaining—
Zosia was his best courier and she
Was needed for the resistance.

To the end of his life, Edelman
Remembered the girl he had
Chosen to pass over to Death
How the numbers were not in her favor.

DIRT DUST DINGINESS AND CONTAMINATION

Lying here mastered by a fit of oncoming flu,
I study the dingy yellow walls, the struggle
of the cream-trimmed woodwork to be
brighter—instead of flushed, fleshed with the history
that browns every least thing in this ancient conurbation.

I feel it moving inside my skin, dragging the murdered
queens within the stage of my brain, squirting me
with returning plague, Victorian miasma,
the nightmare bodies hidden within warped cupboards—
bloodless and faded like the severed thumb
of that famous De Witte in the city museum of the Hague.
Hung. Hustled and hacked by a mob. Dumped in a vitrine
full of blander objects, the thumb still shrivels in its own box.

In London the lemons have too many pips.
The here of here began too many centuries ago.
Everything a too-much swarming memory,
a dinginess, an old-speak clinging to *sticking plaster*
instead of *bandaid*.. Stepping off the #10 bus,
you may *Alight here for the British Museum.*

In Jane's country bedroom the bright lemon walls,
the white chenille cover pulled over her yielding bed
streaky with northern sunshine, while outside
her broad window the gleaming washes of snow.
Hills of Vermont. Nothing especially high.
In the Cabot Village Store the old joke applies.
Ask: *How many Vermonters does it take
to change a light bulb?* Reply: *One to change it;
another to talk about how good the old one was.*

We too love the old, even the old across the Atlantic…
On the Piccadilly Line, on the Victoria,

in the brown, the black, and the blue stations,
the smell of old wet coal suffuses the low
tunneling passages, from which the hump-backed
cars emerge to roar at us, the dull-coated mice
quickening on the tracks below our feet.

In New York rats pop out of rubbish, along gutters
beside the demolished buildings making way
for the new. I see, I pause, in fear of them. My natal
city quite old; the traces of Europe—Asia too—stick
like sticking plaster, the rot between Manhattan boards
as stale, corrupt, contagious as any other. You
cannot rub, wipe off, erase or diminish the past.

Daily I rise to pencil the London listings—finding
the latest Jacobean oddment played by candlelight,
plus the girl who says Juliet's lines as if the thought
had sprung to her lips that minute—or where
the Hamlet-browed pianist sways before me,
a whole well-loved concerto in the tumble
of his hair and the flash of his hands.
               If Europeans did not invent *I castrati,*
it was here—on continent and island, here—even
the young Haydn barely escaped the knife—where
in church and opera house the voices of damaged children
grown to brittle-boned men most brilliantly rang.

My ears, my feet move with the crowds past Holborn,
St. Martin-in-the-fields, to cross Trafalgar Square,
passing demonstrators, monuments—assailed
by a notable waft of sewage coming briefly
past St. Pancras on the way to the British Library—
rumbles, squeals, sirens, the hissing traffic
of the oil-soaked Now. Ecstasy is something
any animal could know, but it takes
the human to think up purity and betray it.

Animals, Too

Animals too come clothed
although unlike us
they have no liberty
to take their furs or feathers off

until death

when the flayed
burst thing on the highway
or in the low hedge
wrynecked and dangling
insults
what they truly are

how could they so let themselves
be seen

At night ahead of us
the yellow headlights of our car
form a moving stage
the fox steps onto   then off

forepaws and hind paws
floating the magnificent
burden of his brush
into the brush

a deer crosses

while just
at the bottom edge of sight
the velvety woodchuck

lifts his head, even

as his eyes look away
never meeting ours

WHITE MAGNOLIA
for R.D.O.

in June, one by one, the floppy
blooms of our white magnolia
unfastened, each
a crumpled hanky
tied too loosely to its twig

and then we heard from you, dear friend,
telling us how you over-heard
your wife and daughter on the phone,
from whom the cries had broken—two cries
in wild
ascending grief—*Oh no, oh no, oh no*—

from the one, and then the distant
heavy sobbing from the other

I walked out for the mail
but the footing was so bad
the mud glistening like chocolate
in the ruts where spring flooding
had gouged the road so deeply

in the middle of it
a boulder-sized hole like a bared eye-socket

"Human Voices Wake Us and We Drown"

For example, Minnesota summer,
Rachel sinking into the back seat,
her slight, ten-year-old body
oddly wrung by the random
baritone of a road-worker
his head filling the car window
while he told us about work stoppage ahead

One resonant voice—an unarmed self
inconsequent words lashed to it
thrilled and punished I hear it
driven across the loud streets
the dead and the dear voices sounding
their intermittences in my helpless ears—

the cling, the clang, the ringing
loss of their known notes

Once, cutting across 9th Street
near Pearl Paint, the unmistakable
timbre of Hollis Frampton's big voice,
at that time unheard for several years
the abiding full of him
coming into view seconds later

ours now only in echo

Litter of instances
each with its soul-popping weight

Like a person drowning
                    soon
I will hear you, see you—
dear ones—you who will be there
still binding me to all the others not

Hollis Frampton, Film-Maker

i
Not for the first time I've thought of how
you lay a curse like maggots to feed on my poems
as you stood there swaying, dead drunk, saying
goodbye in the Kings Highway station, dawn
loosed through the borough of Brooklyn,
which you had loyally got to, crossing from
train to train, all the way from 84 Walker.

But the shock and sting of it I never forgot.

What drew you to us? The aura
of our precocious domesticity, which you
half enviously, half wistfully wise-cracked
was the smell of pee-pot and sour milk.

We had two babies, the first
in our chain of friends, of whom other things
besides progeny had been expected.

Cooking up the good messes that we fed to you,
along with the booze you provided—
for which we certainly did not have the money—
maybe we were your real life,
as you would be our first real dead.

So massively clever, within a group of clever boys.
The spontaneous limericks. The Hopkins parody:
Let hiccup hop-skip-jumpkin bumpkins bruise
Verse which by rot feet, in jerk work scans.
Move I'll not, lurch leg, in bold botch bard's shoes…

ii
Hollis is coming! Hollis is here!
We called to each other in great excitement—

as you entered our college town
in the Studebaker convertible, pedals mounted

just below thc wheel, driving
standing up around Tappan Square
a charioteer in the saddle of a barely tamed beast.

iii
When did the word *glamour* have its rise and fall?
The sheen of brain light: its radiant lure.
At the end of your days too often lit.

Hollis: in intimacy. But oftener Framp.
You had an incredibly loud voice,
which you could dial down
to telling softness: an actor's instrument.

One eye blue, and one eye brown. The pale
near-translucent skin, narrow shoulders,
a white, vulnerable neck rising out of them—
big head and very big mouth, into which, to amuse
our growing babies, you contrived to stuff
your whole fist. Then twitch your large, funny ears...

In a yellowed issue of *October* I come upon
your piece on Eadward Muybridge and cry.

iv
Shattered liver, gone kidneys, and then lung cancer
overtaking that formidable brain. You were
always more fragile than we knew.

That time I read my early poems for you—
you rendered judgment almost indulgently,
a summary murmur yoking
peanut butter chicken and bad poetry.

Now I take the smart with my own indulgence:
following your master Ez, you were the one
who dubbed Virginia Woolf "That chattering female."
As for my snub, I see it flowed from a vast
and distant tenderness: a lot applied
to Art Eternal, with a little left over, for me.

v
You got us wrong, Hollis.
Who we all were or what we were
still in the making, even now.

Once you proposed that we all live together
in some hangar of a Manhattan loft you'd found.
Once you took out your camera and filmed me
as I hopped around and talked so quickly
in the rapid speech you took for my comic sign:

in your film I wear my favorite dress.
The film is six minutes long and has a title:
I recognized it once, when I looked it up.

vi
The question of your movies.
Describing them I have bored so many people.
Take, I would say, *Zorn's Lemma*—

After the rapid, exquisite shuffle of your alphabet:
the quiet sweetness of the final walk
through a snowy field, the camera
never moving, as two tiny people—
and the restless cursor of their leaping dog—
trudge from bottom to top
while the screen holds still.

How you loved it when the loft projector
switched on—the oblong of the screen a pan

of gleaming milk, or did you favor the beam
of light crossing the room, a dust-moted buzzing cone?
I trouble myself to remember more exactly.

Your mouth, half open in epigram,
your white, thin fingers holding the cigarette,
its lethal smoke trailing upwards.

THE AFTERLIFE

I don't believe in the afterlife.
Maybe you could, if as a child like me
you had looked with averted rather than
fierce eyes at the splayed roadkill,
grieving over my dog Skippy as he
lay there indisputably dead.

Dead looks like dead.
Without life. Absolutely stirless.
So fast come the sightless eyes.

We buried him in the raspberry
brambles of the back yard.
With ceremony.

Looking past the flesh,
what did I see?   Filming
inside my head, to fix
all the moments of Dead—
where frame by frame they roll,
shudder, and quicken into Alive?

A sort of resurrection.
Be careful when you make your God
memory: he too
will fade at the edges and go black.

THE WORKS

London barely works. Does England work?
While it waits for Nick the plumber,
our sink is sudsing a tea-colored brown,
as it clogs like the red metal pachyderms
plodding trunk to tail past Euston Station, moving
me towards you in fits and starts, pothole
by pothole, roadwork blocking all paths, day
dropping its light from the fronts of old buildings
bravely holding up their crumbling corners.

Down into the furious, jammed footwork
of sidewalk and street, I wince past a fast stroller,
or blink as an elbow or backpack flicks away
just before it collides with my nose—as the canny
driver of car or bus loops at the last minute,
dodging a crash at the intersection—while
a courteous black man stands three feet
from where I teeter on the curb,
hollering and offering me his arm—
"Come on, Mama, you can do it!"

O my friends! The exhilaration of being
in a few hours, together: the gift of seeing you,
one rising from the ranks of the dying,
along with the one who lives with me, he, too,
risen from the self-same ranks—I dare not
repeat the too-fresh details of his danger—
nor remember too clearly those of mine—

In your familiar rooms,
we five get to look at each other:
one whose eyes dodged blindness,
another whose cancer reached down
and shamelessly touched his private parts,

we see, we hear—like a tribe of Lazarus
we touch each other, bussing lip or cheek
lightly—not wanting to tempt our luck,
we swallow our wine, eat salad, and break bread,
resting awhile from traffic
before the signal moves us on.

TIMOR MORTIS

Past midnight I enter the church of our bed
seeking the smell and feel of you
your flesh tremoring
before you quieten and slide into sleep again

you are not fully wakened and yet
you reach for me

the rattle then stops of your breath
rousing the fear that my light, my
hours, too—
no longer advance
but merely impend   Can you

not take away the little beast
gripping my shoulder whose

lengthening claws
dig deep

IV

THE SWIMMER
for Barry

1
THE STROKE

Of January's two faces, neither
proved your friend. When you
picked up the *Times*, its squirrelly
letters tricked you; dropping it,
you covered your face with your hands,
and said *I'm in a bad way*—consenting
to go to the hospital.
                              Such hope
at first—then deeper and deeper
into speechlessness. I read
the newspaper aloud, Matt shaved you,
Rachel brought soup, and I
brought the deceptively harmless
raspberries you ate so greedily and no doubt
aspirated, as your swallowing
got worse and worse.
                              I played you
soave sia il vento—Mozart's mezzos
have always ravished you—but the reedy
cellphone irritated, and you made me
shut those lyric voices down.
                              By February,
you were still up for Hopkins—long-faced, this
slender Jesuit, at 5'4" a mere two inches taller
than Keats—he bends to the dying
husk of the *hardy-handsome* blacksmith,
whom *Sickness broke*...My tongue
slows for the intricate sonnet, our eyes fill—
we feel the last rite, the *sweet ransom*
the little priest has tendered—*Thy tears
that touched my heart...poor Felix Randal*: and yet
in the large music of the close, it is
the man at the forge mastering

the flame, and the giant animal,
who tower in all their pagan might:

When thou at the random grim forge, powerful amidst peers,
Didst fettle for the great grey drayhorse his bright and battering sandal!

Sleepily, you note how cleverly *Randal* rhymes with *sandal.*

2
THE POET

You were daily shamed by what you could not do.
Even as occasionally from the page the right word
tipped into view.
                        Once, quizzed by a doctor
to identify me, you recited the whole string
of my maiden and marital tags, and grinning wickedly
at your interlocutor, called it *her secret, ineffable Name.*

You grabbed your own book of poems
from my hands, and putting it in front of your face,
misreading the title, declared it a fake,
a book of parodies...

Trying to match a mood, I read from one of your own poems:

> *The presumption that I need a shepherd amuses me*
> *And the presumption of shepherds enrages me.*
> *I don't need staff or rod. I know I'll die.*

You asked me *Who wrote that?*
You did, I said. And gradually, you told me
how the piece came to be written.

Your last visitor in one long poem,
which I read back to you in its multi-planed
entirety, morphs into a sinister double:

> *my allegedly stillborn brother with my own face*
> *and he seemed to bless me...*
> *I knew the rites for welcoming strangers*
> *and blessed him in return and Ha, Ha,*
> *he was not a priest, not my brother, but the Angel of Death*
> *come to play with me, to disassemble my heart.*

3
Hands

I think of his sister caressing his hands—
What beautiful nails he has—those hands
that knew every secret of my body. Strong
but not remarkable in their shaping—merely

owning the grace with which he used them
as the flags of his soul. Out of the water
they rise in those photos I took—back stroke,
flare of the chill lake water behind them,
the white spray of his movement—he wrote,

> *Forgetting the dangerous weight of his body*
> *on the calm skin of the lake, he swims*
> *on his back in the female receptive position,*
> *face to the bright sky, thin clouds*
> *vaporizing fast in the sun's brilliance*
> *afloat in nothing, and the purposeful*
> *seeming union of atoms supporting his weight...*
> *ready*
> *to drift in the water and air and light.*

Nightly,

from the hospital bed, his fingers fluttered goodbye—
after spoon-feeding his supper to him—his mouth
would open like a trusting child's—but then
like the swimmer's, his hand flung back: enough.
I came to put full plates of food away.
That expressive finger would crook:
Come here, do this, do that, for me.

And nightly I abandoned him, wave, wave...

4
THE HOSPITAL

Get me out of here,
you said to Bob.
When they offered you morphine:
They're trying to murder me.
You knew your father's peaceful exit
came through morphine, but
O my darling! You strained to resist. *I'm*
in front of the firing squad, you said.

From when you still could write,
an unfinished poem first asks, then answers:
Who is driving down the road
a curve or two away not visible
from here...a messenger for me
from an unknown power that I must welcome.

The wrathful motions of escape!
Twice at least you ripped out the iv,
moved incessantly to tear
from your face the high-flow
oxygen mask keeping you alive—it

made no sense--but to be
disencumbered, you clawed
at the mask, threw off the bed clothes,
wrenched away the device draining
your urine, messed the bed—
delirium. As gently as we could,

we gripped your self-harming wrists,
pushed back your hands:
a dozen times a day
at your instruction, we pleaded
with the aides in their color-coded

dress of service to raise you
in the specially-crimped hospital bed
you hated; slack and small,
a ragdoll in their competent hands,
the sheets their sling, they slid you
upright again. Smacked the pillows
into shape—only to see you heap
at the bottom within minutes.

How lovingly, with what
incomprehensible patience
so many of them treated you, Juan
caressingly calming you
and calling you *Papi*.

The harrowing dullness of the unstoppable
helpless, hopeless routines.

It took so long to stop thinking you would live.
You thought you would live.

5
Why

Evenings when I left you,
the window held the New York sky,
a humming indigo with gridded lights.
From the hospital bed,
your fingers flapped at me their small

resigned *goodbye*—my sweetheart
how you hated the slough
of that bed, poor "windowless monad"
$\qquad\qquad$ departing from it
in anger and terror, even
as in delirium you spun
your crazy jokes, made
witty and precise distinctions
from within those strange
fantastic habitats in which
your mind entrapped you

Why couldn't you die
as others did, with sweetness
and dignity less intermittent, all
your faculties undiminished, pulsing:

the last night you twisted
the sheets and then
my fingers with such
ferocity—*amazing*

the strength of his hands,
the nurse remarked—hurting me
so that I could only

pull away, yelping

6
ENOUGH

In the churning weeks your mind
anchored itself briefly—and you
remembered that we each
had promised to dispatch the other,
when disabled to speak for ourselves:
but in your ultimate suffering,
how bitterly
you gave your power away:
even as your firm voice
assented, and the lawyer
took it down. O my dear

in the days of the last goodbye—
your eyes
so bright
so furious
at dying

Enough—you had said—
very faintly

In misery, I think your teeth
gritted with rage
at the distance from you
of the living

7
THE CRUX

What he fought was raw extinction.
He refused it.
              What is there but dot dot dot…
which is really not, not, and not. The senses
quailing, cutting out—the terrible rigidity, that
massive, useless stillness for those who love you.
A dead human must be burned or buried.
We turn away from the graveside and its busy
cellular dispersals, to the white pain of absence.

You were *pathologically optimistic!*
So often you said that.

All the other struggles had been successful,
and this was just another knot in the string:
you, the doctors, and the hospital
had fought one cancer back—you
were so strong…In California they'd given you
six months to live—and see?
A lucky seven years took you all the way
to chemo for a new cancer,
in which a catastrophic stroke
had broken you:
              Your oncologist over the phone
to me was audibly aghast, because sarcoma
was savaging your body now: the fine
network of ways mending the stroke
irrelevant to the new cancer swallowing you.

One protocol countermanded the other.
There wasn't a force path through—day after day,
then week after week, until March came
and marched you away. You

did not choose to go. You
were a person who died. My person.

8
GOLDEN LADS AND GIRLS ALL MUST

When I was finally alone with you,
I bent my face, first drawing
aside the towels and blankets
soaking up the edematous weeping
of your swollen arms—those punctures
at the wrist, signaling the multiple
intravenous incursions, swabbed
away—but in that stubble which I had kissed,
even in your hardest—and angriest—days,
your own lips were too weak
to press back at the last.
                                  This face
now arches from the pillow, the nose
painfully sharp and beaking.
The bony ridges of your temples
strain upward from the skull, cradling
the eyelids that fluttered, and did,
at my touch, refuse to close,
above the loud
and terrible blackness
of your mouth agape: a fissure

from which immense consciousness
was draining in its unknown
mysterious pace. You

were no longer you. But
on the flat plane of your white
dead belly, my lips
touched the shrunken penis,
still cased in that efficient plastic trap
leading urine off to its
discreet hose; at the junction
of the legs which led you

to the beautiful motions of your long life,
where lay the source
of my deepest and oldest pleasures—there
I greeted us;
discharging the body once mine to love.

9
THE BARDO

Us, we, our: within the minute
of your final breath, these pronouns
lost the power of the future.

Lying here. Alone
in *our* double bed, in *our*
apartment in which invisible
approaching steps behind
the closed front door will never
unite to be *us* again. I whisper
out loud to him but the air
is punishingly silent--
                              for exactly
two precious weeks, he hovered
near me; I could feel
him: and then the *we* left.

Reading hungrily I see
that the Bardo ripens
for 49 days and then the flesh
recycles into other life.

He stopped being.
As Annie once said to us primly—
When I am dead my body
will have something better to do
than to be a person.

O yes, Annie! I try to see him
transformed as bear, cougar,
or owl, maybe eagle, or fox on the run—
as flight; as flash, or brightness—
but only the brightness holds.

Big spirit, his going was difficult—but

in the ripe persistence of objects,
in the electric charges of memory—

here he is: his very glasses
still folded beside the tv;
the tips of his moccasins peeping
from under the dresser,
where Marilyn set them carefully
beyond her mop, turning him
into a person levitating—obscured
but upright—within my bedroom furniture.

10
Where Are You?

How can you be dead?
It's so irritating.
You're like the bird
In the Monty Python sketch
E's not dead, e's only sleeping.

Only sleeping somewhere I can't find you

I made a terrible mistake
I've misplaced you

Or you are hiding from me—
it makes me cross—

You were certainly dead
when I left you.
That was no living person
fixed on the hospital bed,
a mason jar of flowers on the sill
a spray of rosemary, thyme
and lavender that Rachel
tried to close your fingers over

so that dying you would have
something nice to smell.

But you were certainly there,
although unmoving, in the last sight
I had of you on earth.

I told the nurse I wanted to leave
before they zipped you into the body bag.
I did not want to see

how you went from person into thing
as the zipper zipped: after
all the others had left, I said
my goodbye and crossed the room—

you lay so still behind me—but
between then and now,
where did you go?

11
WEEPING

There was weeping of course
the moment you died—beside
the roaring in my head,
Bob's hard, broken sobbing,
your son-in-law
who truly loved you--

And yet it was all natural
I couldn't help saying to myself:
soon enough
before I wish it
I will follow you.

Look at you! Look at you!
My young and beautiful boy...
I close my old woman's eyes, lean
back, and plummet
through the decades to where
the two of us began—

quick, lithe and randy, you could
put it to me anywhere,
or any time: I did respond.

Tears rise, as the full weight of you
slams into memory:
Closer, closer, you would murmur
as we clung to each other—
even in the late years
our bodies igniting at a touch.

O my darling! I hear how
I weep for myself—unmended

the wasted hours, stupid arguments,
blind bickering, misdirected anger—
I in tumult, you seething...
I could have
paused. Turned to you.
Sometimes I did.

12
WHAT HAPPENS

What happens when dying body goes to dead?
How to find the exact point
in that flail of seconds
during which extinction came…

And why should the very *When* matter?
It's not a good question.
I only ask it because I am lashed to it—

my dumb mind in its hopeless grinding
thinks that if I can
go to the place where I lost you
I could make you pick up being again.

So much helpless force wills it—
The habit of loving you keeps
trickling through the system with nowhere to go.
The habit of you on my skin. Your voice

still coming through distant tunnels at me.
Some weeks after you died the precious
sight of you bursting through the bathroom door
and as I joyfully called your name, your face
splintered and disappeared.

13
HELLO YOUNG LOVERS

Gertrude Lawrence, middle-aged governess
in lace mitts and crinoline, calls to me from YouTube
in that sweet, clotted, tremulous voice,
her uncertain pitch buoyed by the soft
orchestral pillow, where her rising notes
accentuate not loss but the triumph of ownership—

I've had a love of my own—

which I so badly want to hear:
coming away from the hospital, crossing
my city streets alone, and riding my city buses
alone, wincing at the ordinary, healthy couples
hand and hand, unconscious of their luck.

I remember, the singer warbles, *and I always will—*
The misty, English hillside where she, Anna,
and her Tom looked out to sea.
The couple they were. The love they bore.

I've had a love... of my own. Her mortal
voice in a kind of hiccup, or sob, breaking,
before she hits *of my own*...she is
in steamy Thailand, once Siam—

like you, one of the young lovers
in her show is burnt to ashes—
although the barbaric king has ordered
that unlike you he is not dead
when the burning takes place.

Your lips tickle my ear
whispering something tender to me
If I say it out loud

and blow on the memory
too many times, little by little
my breath will destroy it

14
HEALING

She promised me that my *Was-ness,*
my face to the past,
would change to an *Is-ness,*
as I carry forward into the life without you.
I cannot see it—I cannot see it!

And besides, doesn't the vaunted
healing merely mean
a scabbing over
that makes a virtue of indifference?

Crumbling forgetfulness that takes away
the scorch of loss.
If the burn lasts, the memory lasts:
what else can I want but my pain?

Talking to myself I still talk to you.
There is no ending to the poems
I will write for you, writing you
back into my life,
one fleshless page after the other.

All that I have
one fleshless page after the other.

About the Author

Lorrie Goldensohn's work has always split between writing prose and poetry, and writing about reading prose and poetry. Many articles on fiction writers like Virginia Woolf and Natalia Ginsburg have been published in journals and anthologies, as well as dozens of articles on poetry and war literature. Her critical studies include *Elizabeth Bishop: The Biography of a Poetry* (nominated for a Pulitzer Prize), and *Dismantling Glory: 20th Century English and American War Poets*. She has taught at Goddard, Hampshire, and Vassar Colleges, and currently divides her time between Manhattan and Cabot, Vermont.

Fomite

Writing a review on social media sites for readers will help the progress of independent publishing. To submit a review, go to the book page on any of the sites and follow the links for reviews. Books from independent presses rely on reader-to-reader communications.

For more information or to order any of our books, visit:
http://www.fomitepress.com/our-books.html

More poetry from Fomite...
Anna Blackmer — *Hexagrams*
L. Brown — *Loopholes*
Sue D. Burton — *Little Steel*
Christine Butterworth-McDermott — *Evelyn As*
Christine Butterworth-McDermott — *The Spellbook of Fruit and Flowers*
David Cavanagh— *Cycling in Plato's Cave*
Rajnesh Chakrapani — *The Repetition of Exceptional Weeks*
James Connolly — *Picking Up the Bodies*
Benjamin Dangl — *A World Where Many Worlds Fit*
Greg Delanty — *Behold the Garden*
Greg Delanty — *Loosestrife*
Mason Drukman — *Drawing on Life*
J. C. Ellefson — *Foreign Tales of Exemplum and Woe*
Anna Faktorovich — *Improvisational Arguments*
Peter Fortunato — *World Headquarters*
Barry Goldensohn — *Snake in the Spine, Wolf in the Heart*
Barry Goldensohn — *The Hundred Yard Dash Man*
Barry Goldensohn — *The Listener Aspires to the Condition of Music*
Barry Goldensohn — *Visitors Entrance*
Lorrie Goldensohn — *Little Fish*
R. L. Green — *When You Remember Deir Yassin*
KJ Hannah Greenberg — *Beast There—Don't That*
Kevin Hadduck — *Beloved Brother, Beloved Sister*
John Hawkins — *Mirror to Mirror*
Christopher Heffernan — *[laughter]*
Gail Holst-Warhaft — *Lucky Country*
Judith Kerman — *Definitions*
Yahia Lababidi — *Quarantine Notes*
Joseph Lamport — *Enlightenment*
Raymond Luczak — *A Babble of Objects*

Fomite

Fomite

Made in the USA
Columbia, SC
29 September 2024

42651241R00064